Finding This Day's Joy:
A Year of Living Gratefully

Gina Prosch

Lohman Hills Creative, LLC
PO Box 105552
Jefferson City, Missouri 65110
USA

ISBN: 978-1539454861

Visit the author at www.GinaProsch.com

Finding This Day's Joy: A Year of Living Gratefully

Gina Prosch

Introduction

Over the course of a lifetime there are lots of lost keys.

Lost purses and wallets.

Lost favorite socks.

And lots and lots of lost tools and beloved toys.

Those lost things send you on a search, and—most of the time—you find what you're looking for.

More or less.

Lots of times, I'm surprised where I find things.

The lost phone tucked in the couch cushion.

The car keys in the washing machine.

The book I was reading on the deck is found outside in the garden? Really? I have no idea how that happened.

But also, I'm surprised by the multitide of additional things I didn't expect to find.

Looking for the phone, I found a five dollar bill.

Searching for the car keys: that favorite sock.

Tracking down the book—a blooming dafodil I hadn't noticed before.

The same holds true for things that happen in life—search for something long enough, keep your eyes open wide enough, and you'll probably find it.

And much more alongside.

Search for pain, suffering, and reasons to be angry. I don't have to tell you—look for it and you'll find plenty.

But is simple joy so much more elusive? If we look, can we find it? And more besides?

• • • • •

One day while I scrolled through my Facebook feed, looking at all the perfect lives, admittedly searching for ways I didn't measure up and feeling more than a little bit sorry for myself, the cat came running through the house.

When she went from carpeting to hardwood flooring she took a header and slid into the wall.

This was immediately followed with one of those: "Nobody saw that, right?" looks.

It totally cracked me up.

I glanced down, and Facebook asked me, "What's on your mind?" so I typed:

This Day's Joy: Watching the cat run through the house and try to turn a quick corner on hardwood floors.

The next day I decided to look for something else:

Watching the zinnias & cosmos in the flower garden bob their heads in the breeze.

And the day after that:

Homemade, fresh-from-the-oven baking powder biscuits - all golden brown - with homemade raspberry jam melting over the top.

And the day after that:

Knowing there are fresh, crisp sheets waiting for you when you slip into bed tonight.

Each day I looked for something good that happened that day, and by golly I found something.

There was always at least one thing...sometimes two or three.

Sometimes I had whole lists of wonderful things that happened during the day and it was hard to decide.

I kept it up for a week, then a month, finally an entire year.

Now it's been several years, and every single day I search for a small wonderful thing.

Something I'm grateful for, something inexpensive, something requiring only awareness of its existence.

What I've noticed—and what I hope you will notice, too—is that knowing I'll need something that fits the bill for "this day's joy" means I start compiling a mental list first thing in the morning throughout the whole day.

This Day's Joy?

What could it be?

A new bar of soap that smells really good, a fresh box of Lucky Charms™, that first cup of morning coffee, or perfectly browned toast with melty butter.

Maybe it's realizing I had my shirt buttoned up wrong *before* I got to the client meeting.

By lunchtime there are always a few things on the list, and by supper, a few more.

A terrific waiter at lunch, a quick but glorious afternoon catnap, or a "green lights all the way" drive home.

During the evening?

A gorgeous sunset, the smell of the mimosa tree heavy in the summer air, or clean sheets on the bed at night.

I find what I'm looking for.

In abundance.

The opposite holds true. If I spend the entire day looking for things to complain about, things that are less than perfect, things that really grind my gears...well, I will find them!

Someone cut me off in traffic, I dripped salsa down my shirtfront at lunch, the stupid grocery cart wheel got stuck halfway through the store, then the clerk put the watermelon on top of the bread, and when I finally got home...what do you mean we're out of toilet paper????

I can make a list of those things too.

But, at the end of the day I realized I'd rather have a list of wonderful things to think about than unpleasant things to think about.

It doesn't mean the bad things in life go away.

It doesn't mean I put my head in the sand and pretend they didn't happen.

I know all too well that bad things do indeed happen, but they don't have to rule the day.

• • • • •

Finding This Day's Joy: A Year of Living Gratefully is a mark-it-up-journal designed to be a hands-on tool to inspire you to look for — and find — the joy that's always nearby.

Whether you tuck this journal into your briefcase or bag, set it beside your favorite chair for evening contemplation, or leave it on your bedside table for use last thing at night, the important thing is to make a habit of reflecting on the day in a positive way.

When you make time every day to look for This Day's Joy, you also have an opportunity to reframe daily annoyances into something better, more positive and uplifting.

"Someone cut me off in traffic" makes me realize *I have excellent defensive driving skills and avoided an accident.*

"I dripped salsa down my shirtfront at lunch" transforms into *I had a scarf in my coat pocket and it covered up the salsa drip* or maybe it means *I finally have proof that carrying a stain stick in my purse isn't that OCD after all.*

"What do you mean we're out of toilet paper?" becomes *an evening drive to the store where you're treated to the most beautiful moonrise.*

Learning how to positively reframe small things on a daily basis isn't just putting on rose colored glasses and ignoring reality; instead, it's a way of shifting your awareness, it's a tool for becoming emotionally resilient.

• • • • •

Begin actively looking for things to be grateful for. Begin transforming negatives into opportunities.

- Start this journal on January 1st with the new year.
- Or on your birthday day (for your own uniquely personal new year).
- Start it on the first day of a new school year.
- Or an anniversary.
- Start now.

To aid you on your search for *Finding This Day's Joy*, there are cues to jog your thinking and help you take notice of what's around you.

There are things that are obvious: great tastes, amazing smells, and delicious flavors.

Then there are the surprises. Surprises don't have to be elaborate gifts or gestures that don't come around all that often. Surprises are also the little things that often go unnoticed: the penny you found on the sidewalk, the person ahead of you in the fast food drive-thru who pays for your coffee, or the person who opens the door for you because your hands are full.

There are the wonderful memories — something kind that someone said or did for you, a piece of advice someone gave to you, something that reminds you of your very best times — things that pop into your mind as remembrances of times past.

• • • • •

So don't wait around hoping to find joy tomorrow.
Go out and seize the day.

Find joy today, then squeeze every bit of happiness out of every single day all year long.

You will be amazed at what you find.

Finding This Day's Joy

Today's Date: 9/23/2021

This Day's Joy:
Seeing a humble smile
on my son michael.
something I have not.
seen in a long time

A favorite childhood memory
putting fall decorations out
thinking apple pumpkin

Something you're looking forward to next week
Sunflower field

A positive reframe — one way today could have been worse
I kept on the joy of my life
not the worry.

Today's Date: 9/24/2021

This Day's Joy:

DROplets of Rain water
Hanging on fence -
looks like crystal-sparkle
gems - Beautiful

One reason you wouldn't trade places with anyone

I Know what I have - Jesus
I don't Know what others have

An expression of generosity

cooking lamb chops for my son

A pleasing fragrance

Morning Coffee

fresh fall Air

Today's Date: 9/25/2021

This Day's Joy:

• Praying for family, friends, & the whole world waiting for an oil change at Lou's Auto

Something delicious to eat

Sausage Pizza from Krispy's

Something silly that never fails to make you laugh

children on the beach

Your favorite thing about waking up each day

NEW BEGINNINGS-

Today's Date: 9/26/2021

This Day's Joy:

SunFlower Field

A *sign of the changing seasons you enjoy*

Colors of fall leaves / TREES
smell of spices /
Pumpkins and apples

Something that made you happy today

Shhhh, don't tell — a sneaky indulgence

Finding This Day's Joy

Today's Date: __9/28/2021__

This Day's Joy:

my son cooking & preparing food.

Something new you tried recently

easy does it / Being with me.

Something you noticed in a quiet moment

Sound of life / Breathe
I am OK.

The best thing that happened during the past week

cooking with michael

Today's Date: 9/29/2021

This Day's Joy:
Back Pain is much
Better

A happy surprise
Phone calls from 2 friends
who really care.

A moment that soothed your soul
listeing to music Stan 99.1

Describe a happy, memorable event from high school
Making captain of cheerleaders

Today's Date: 9/30/2021

This Day's Joy:
TO WAKE with more
Peace - Less Pain

The best thing about you today
I listened to, Donna Summer
& Abba and danced and had
a great time

Something that felt good
TO TAKE A walk and
appreciate my surrondings

A favorite springtime holiday memory
VAcations - Birthdays.
CHARleston South Carollina

Today's Date: 10/1/2021

This Day's Joy:

Dancing to Donna Summer
while making Pumpkin Bread
in my kitchen

A quotation that inspires you

Live and Let Live!

A personal luxury — something just for you

Having and Being my own self
and enjoying my alone time

Something nice someone said to you

God Bless You

Today's Date: 10/2/2021

This Day's Joy:

working on Arizona vacation plan

A delicious flavor you enjoy

Broccoli rape / hot sausage / orrichedto
yummy

A few of your favorites things

meditiation in the sunshine

Something you worried about that didn't happen

my Back pain - Gone today

Today's Date: 10/3/2021

This Day's Joy:
A GREAT BEACH DAY
and it is FALL
Allelehuia

You did it! Name a tiny triumph
Get thru the day — no backpain

Something that makes you laugh
Seeing baby walking with
mom in ocean — taking
1st steps

Furry, feathered, or finny friends — a great pet moment
I HAVE NO PETS - But seeing
others with theirs is
comforting

Today's Date: 10/4/2021

This Day's Joy:

TO BE PRESENT IN All
I needed to do

A gorgeous sight to behold

my mom after her hair was
cut / Blown. To see how
Beautiful she is

Three positive words to describe this day

JoyFul - Peaceful Grateful
fearless

A big weight off your shoulders,

Hair was dyed after 2½ months

Today's Date: 10/5/2021

This Day's Joy:

Enjoying my son's stability

The best thing that happened to you during the past week

I got my hair dyed.
Went to Beach in Oct.

Something cozy you enjoy

Cooking with my son and
talking about life.

A positive reframe — choosing a better focus

Let Go when you start to
feel stressed - anger - etc.
Let God.

Today's Date: 10/12/2021

This Day's Joy:
Waking up with little to
no back pain.
10 minute BreathWork-worked
with O Be fitness

A tasty treat you ate today
Homemade applesauce

A goal you achieved
Got correct info on Being A Poll worker
Training necessary

Something you're looking forward to next week
TRAING TO BE A POLL WORKER
Certifiaette good for
2 YEARS

Today's Date: _____

This Day's Joy:

_____

_____

_____

_____

_____

A favorite song from your personal playlist

_____

_____

_____

Something added to or crossed off your bucket list

_____

_____

_____

Something colorful that brightens your day

_____

_____

_____

Today's Date: _____

This Day's Joy:

_____

_____

_____

_____

_____

A favorite vacation memory

_____

_____

_____

Something you wouldn't trade for all the money in the world

_____

_____

_____

A connection with nature that relaxes you

_____

_____

_____

Today's Date: _____

This Day's Joy:

_____

_____

_____

_____

_____

An experience worth remembering

_____

_____

_____

A breath of fresh air

_____

_____

_____

A fun time you had with friends

_____

_____

_____

Today's Date: _____

This Day's Joy:

_____

_____

_____

_____

_____

Something beautiful you encountered

_____

_____

_____

A favorite beverage you enjoyed today

_____

_____

_____

A good thought you like to go to sleep on

_____

_____

_____

Today's Date: _____

This Day's Joy:

_____

_____

_____

_____

_____

A tantalizing smell

_____

_____

_____

A random kindness done by you or for you

_____

_____

_____

Something you're looking forward to this year

_____

_____

_____

Today's Date: _____

This Day's Joy:

_____

_____

_____

_____

_____

A hobby you enjoy

_____

_____

_____

If you could turn back time — a best day ever

_____

_____

_____

The best thing that happened during the past week

_____

_____

_____

Today's Date: _____

This Day's Joy:

_____

_____

_____

_____

_____

A bit of wonderfulness from nature

_____

_____

_____

A few of your favorites things

_____

_____

_____

A compliment – given or received

_____

_____

_____

Today's Date: _____

This Day's Joy:

_____

_____

_____

_____

_____

Paint a word picture of something lovely

_____

_____

_____

Something kind someone said to you

_____

_____

_____

A victory to celebrate

_____

_____

_____

Today's Date: _____

This Day's Joy:

_____

_____

_____

_____

_____

Something yummy you ate

_____

_____

_____

Three positive words to describe your day

_____

_____

_____

A positive reframe — a silver lining to a dark cloud

_____

_____

_____

Today's Date: _____

This Day's Joy:

_____

_____

_____

_____

_____

Something that felt good

_____

_____

_____

A favorite childhood memory

_____

_____

_____

Something you admire in a friend

_____

_____

_____

Today's Date: _____

This Day's Joy:

_____

_____

_____

_____

_____

Something that made you smile

_____

_____

_____

Something you're looking forward to next week

_____

_____

_____

A soul soothing moment

_____

_____

_____

Today's Date: _____

This Day's Joy:

_____

_____

_____

_____

_____

A fun surprise

_____

_____

_____

Dream big! Someplace you'd like to visit someday

_____

_____

_____

If you'd only known — good advice to your childhood self

_____

_____

_____

Today's Date: _____

This Day's Joy:

_____

_____

_____

_____

_____

A fragrance that had you breathing deeply

_____

_____

_____

The best thing to happen today

_____

_____

_____

An indulgence that makes you feel special

_____

_____

_____

Today's Date: _____

This Day's Joy:

_____

_____

_____

_____

_____

A random kindness

_____

_____

_____

Relive a memorable moment

_____

_____

_____

The best thing about you today

_____

_____

_____

Today's Date: _____

This Day's Joy:

_____

_____

_____

_____

_____

A personal luxury that doesn't cost anything

_____

_____

_____

Something funny that happened

_____

_____

_____

A story that inspires you

_____

_____

_____

Today's Date: _____

This Day's Joy:

_____

_____

_____

_____

_____

Something new you tried

_____

_____

_____

Something you admire in a co-worker

_____

_____

_____

Times change. A sign of the season to savor

_____

_____

_____

Today's Date: _____

This Day's Joy:

_____

_____

_____

_____

_____

A happy sound you heard

_____

_____

_____

Your favorite comfort food at the end of a long day

_____

_____

_____

Something you do for an instant unwind

_____

_____

_____

Today's Date: _____

This Day's Joy:

_____

_____

_____

_____

_____

A way you succeeded today

_____

_____

_____

An amazing burst of flavor

_____

_____

_____

A gorgeous sight to behold

_____

_____

_____

Today's Date: _____

This Day's Joy:

_____

_____

_____

_____

_____

Look around and connect with your senses

_____

_____

_____

You wouldn't trade places with anyone else because

_____

_____

_____

Something silly that never fails to make you laugh

_____

_____

_____

Today's Date: _____

This Day's Joy:

_____

_____

_____

_____

_____

A few of your favorites things

_____

_____

_____

A positive reframe — choosing a better focus

_____

_____

_____

The best thing that happened during the past week

_____

_____

_____

Today's Date: _____

This Day's Joy:

_____

_____

_____

_____

_____

Three positive words to describe today

_____

_____

_____

A random kindness you did for someone else

_____

_____

_____

A time you felt a connection with nature

_____

_____

_____

Today's Date: _____

This Day's Joy:

_____

_____

_____

_____

_____

An unexpected positive

_____

_____

_____

Something you're looking forward to next week

_____

_____

_____

A way you were your authentic self

_____

_____

_____

Today's Date: _____

This Day's Joy:

_____

_____

_____

_____

_____

Something you find soothing

_____

_____

_____

A positive reframe — making lemonade from lemons

_____

_____

_____

Something nice someone said to you

_____

_____

_____

Today's Date: _____

This Day's Joy:

_____

_____

_____

_____

_____

A song that always brightens your day

_____

_____

_____

A favorite summer holiday memory

_____

_____

_____

Something you admire in a family member

_____

_____

_____

Today's Date: _____

This Day's Joy:

_____
_____
_____
_____
_____

An experience you wish you could relive

_____
_____
_____

Something that made you smile today

_____
_____
_____

A good thought to go to sleep on

_____
_____
_____

Today's Date: _____

This Day's Joy:

_____

_____

_____

_____

_____

Childhood memories — what made you happy way back when

_____

_____

_____

A reason to give a huge sigh of relief

_____

_____

_____

Something noticable only in a quiet moment

_____

_____

_____

Today's Date: _____

This Day's Joy:

_____

_____

_____

_____

_____

The absolute best thing about your pet

_____

_____

_____

The best thing that happened to you during the past week

_____

_____

_____

Something that made you laugh

_____

_____

_____

Today's Date: _____

This Day's Joy:

_____

_____

_____

_____

_____

Paint a word picture of something lovely in your home

_____

_____

_____

A compliment you gave to someone

_____

_____

_____

A small victory you are working toward right now

_____

_____

_____

Today's Date: _____

This Day's Joy:

_____

_____

_____

_____

_____

Something you worried about that didn't happen

_____

_____

_____

Something refreshing you ate or drank

_____

_____

_____

A positive reframe — a silver lining to a dark cloud

_____

_____

_____

Today's Date: _____

This Day's Joy:

_____
_____
_____
_____
_____

A favorite memory from childhood

_____
_____
_____

Shhhh, don't tell — a sneaky indulgence

_____
_____
_____

If you could turn back time — a best day ever

_____
_____
_____

Today's Date: _____

This Day's Joy:

_____
_____
_____
_____
_____

One positive word to sum up your day

_____
_____
_____

A soul soothing moment

_____
_____
_____

Your favorite outdoor activity

_____
_____
_____

Today's Date: _____

This Day's Joy:

_____

_____

_____

_____

_____

A favorite song from your personal playlist

_____

_____

_____

A fun time you had with friends

_____

_____

_____

A happy surprise

_____

_____

_____

Today's Date: _____

This Day's Joy:

_____

_____

_____

_____

_____

Something you wouldn't trade for all the money in the world

_____

_____

_____

A taste that left you wanting more

_____

_____

_____

The reason you love your all-time-favorite television show

_____

_____

_____

Today's Date: _____

This Day's Joy:

_____

_____

_____

_____

_____

The best thing about right here, right now

_____

_____

_____

Something you're looking forward to next week

_____

_____

_____

The best thing that happened to you so far this year

_____

_____

_____

Today's Date: _____

This Day's Joy:

_____

_____

_____

_____

_____

Something beautiful you saw

_____

_____

_____

Describe a memorable event you participated in

_____

_____

_____

A personal luxury — something just for you

_____

_____

_____

Today's Date: _____

This Day's Joy:

_____
_____
_____
_____
_____

Advice you'd love to give your younger self

_____
_____
_____

A happy surprise

_____
_____
_____

The best thing you smelled all day

_____
_____
_____

Today's Date: _____

This Day's Joy:

_____

_____

_____

_____

_____

An event you're looking forward to next year

_____

_____

_____

Something you really like about you

_____

_____

_____

A random kindness done by you or for you

_____

_____

_____

Today's Date: _____

This Day's Joy:

_____

_____

_____

_____

_____

Something kind someone said to you

_____

_____

_____

A gorgeous sight to behold

_____

_____

_____

A goal you worked for and finally achieved

_____

_____

_____

Today's Date: _____

This Day's Joy:

_____

_____

_____

_____

_____

Your favorite comfort food at this time of year

_____

_____

_____

A quotation that inspires you

_____

_____

_____

A positive reframe — choosing a better focus

_____

_____

_____

Today's Date: _____

This Day's Joy:

_____

_____

_____

_____

_____

Someone you'd love to talk to

_____

_____

_____

Something that felt good to touch

_____

_____

_____

A happy childhood memory

_____

_____

_____

Today's Date: _____

This Day's Joy:

_____

_____

_____

_____

_____

Added to or crossed off your bucket list

_____

_____

_____

The best thing that happened to you during the past week

_____

_____

_____

Something that makes your mouth water

_____

_____

_____

Today's Date: _____

This Day's Joy:

_____

_____

_____

_____

_____

Three positive words to describe this day

_____

_____

_____

Something guaranteed to make you smile

_____

_____

_____

The best thing about playing or watching your favorite sport

_____

_____

_____

Today's Date: _____

This Day's Joy:

_____

_____

_____

_____

_____

Childhood fantasties — something you dreamed about as a kid

_____

_____

_____

A few of your favorite things

_____

_____

_____

Something that never fails to cheer your mood

_____

_____

_____

74

Today's Date: _____

This Day's Joy:

_____

_____

_____

_____

_____

Something you're looking forward to next year

_____

_____

_____

A reason you admire someone

_____

_____

_____

Something funny that happened this week

_____

_____

_____

75

Today's Date: _____

This Day's Joy:

_____

_____

_____

_____

_____

Something you're looking forward to next month

_____

_____

_____

A way to show yourself empathy

_____

_____

_____

A connection you experienced with nature and enjoyed

_____

_____

_____

Today's Date: _____

This Day's Joy:

_____

_____

_____

_____

_____

Something new you learned recently

_____

_____

_____

An act of generosity you were grateful to receive

_____

_____

_____

A weight off your shoulders

_____

_____

_____

Today's Date: _____

This Day's Joy:

_____

_____

_____

_____

_____

A quality you appreciate in a friend or family member

_____

_____

_____

Something silly that never fails to make you laugh

_____

_____

_____

Describe something memorable you did as a child

_____

_____

_____

Today's Date: _____

This Day's Joy:

_____

_____

_____

_____

_____

Word pictures. Describe something you see every day that's lovely

_____

_____

_____

Savor a sign of the season – what do you enjoy right now

_____

_____

_____

The best thing that happened during the past week

_____

_____

_____

Today's Date: _____

This Day's Joy:

_____

_____

_____

_____

_____

Your favorite decoration or spot in your home

_____

_____

_____

A positive reframe — make lemonade from lemons

_____

_____

_____

A breakthrough you achieved through your own efforts

_____

_____

_____

Today's Date: _____

This Day's Joy:

_____

_____

_____

_____

_____

Something delicious you ate

_____

_____

_____

A soul soothing moment

_____

_____

_____

Childhood fantasies — something you pretended as a kid

_____

_____

_____

81

Today's Date: _____

This Day's Joy:

_____

_____

_____

_____

_____

An enticing smell

_____

_____

_____

Music that makes you happy

_____

_____

_____

If you could turn back time — a best day ever

_____

_____

_____

Today's Date: _____

This Day's Joy:

_____

_____

_____

_____

_____

A reason you wouldn't trade places with anyone else

_____

_____

_____

A way you enjoy connecting with nature

_____

_____

_____

Shhhh, don't tell — a sneaky indulgence

_____

_____

_____

Finding This Day's Joy

Today's Date: _____

This Day's Joy:

_____

_____

_____

_____

_____

Give your best advice to yourself at seven-years-old

_____

_____

_____

The best part of waking up

_____

_____

_____

Two positive words to describe this day

_____

_____

_____

84

Today's Date: _____

This Day's Joy:

_____

_____

_____

_____

_____

Three of your favorites things

_____

_____

_____

Something nice someone said to you

_____

_____

_____

A favorite fall holiday memory

_____

_____

_____

Today's Date: _____

This Day's Joy:

_____

_____

_____

_____

_____

The best thing about you today

_____

_____

_____

Your favorite item of clothing in your closet

_____

_____

_____

The best thing that happened during the past week

_____

_____

_____

Today's Date: _____

This Day's Joy:

_____

_____

_____

_____

_____

Something that made you really laugh out loud this week

_____

_____

_____

Something you're looking forward to next week

_____

_____

_____

A compliment you gave to someone

_____

_____

_____

Today's Date: _____

This Day's Joy:

_____

_____

_____

_____

_____

Something that never fails to take your breath away

_____

_____

_____

What do you enjoy about still, quiet moments

_____

_____

_____

A breath of fresh air

_____

_____

_____

Today's Date: _____

This Day's Joy:

_____

_____

_____

_____

_____

Describe something worth remembering

_____

_____

_____

A tiny triumph

_____

_____

_____

Something that far exceeded your expectations

_____

_____

_____

Today's Date: _____

This Day's Joy:

_____

_____

_____

_____

_____

A positive reframe — choosing a better focus

_____

_____

_____

Furry, feathered, or finny friends — a great pet moment

_____

_____

_____

A way to relax that you always look forward to

_____

_____

_____

Today's Date: _____

This Day's Joy:

_____

_____

_____

_____

_____

A favorite story you love to tell with family or friends

_____

_____

_____

Something you worried about that didn't happen

_____

_____

_____

A coat or jacket that you look forward to wearing each winter

_____

_____

_____

Today's Date: _____

This Day's Joy:

_____

_____

_____

_____

_____

A delicious hot beverage

_____

_____

_____

A random act of kindness you did for a stranger

_____

_____

_____

Something that used to be scary that isn't any more

_____

_____

_____

Today's Date: _____

This Day's Joy:

_____

_____

_____

_____

_____

The best thing that happened during the past week

_____

_____

_____

Sing a song — a favorite from your personal playlist

_____

_____

_____

The best part of waking up today

_____

_____

_____

Today's Date: _____

This Day's Joy:

_____

_____

_____

_____

_____

A quotation that inspires you

_____

_____

_____

A fun time you had with friends

_____

_____

_____

Something beautiful you encountered unexpectedly

_____

_____

_____

Today's Date: _____

This Day's Joy:

_____

_____

_____

_____

_____

A long-term goal you achieved

_____

_____

_____

Three positive words to describe this day

_____

_____

_____

What wouldn't you trade for all the money in the world

_____

_____

_____

Today's Date: _____

This Day's Joy:

_____

_____

_____

_____

_____

Your favorites book or series of books

_____

_____

_____

Something wonderful you found in nature

_____

_____

_____

A good thought to go to sleep on

_____

_____

_____

Today's Date: _____

This Day's Joy:

_____

_____

_____

_____

_____

A huge relief you experienced recently

_____

_____

_____

A way you relaxed today

_____

_____

_____

A favorite smell at this time of year

_____

_____

_____

Today's Date: _____

This Day's Joy:

_____

_____

_____

_____

_____

If you could be anywhere on earth, you'd be....

_____

_____

_____

A terrific surprise

_____

_____

_____

Paint a word picture of someone you love

_____

_____

_____

Today's Date: _____

This Day's Joy:

_____
_____
_____
_____
_____

Something you're looking forward to next week

_____
_____
_____

A way you exceeded your expectations of yourself

_____
_____
_____

Something that felt good

_____
_____
_____

Today's Date: _____

This Day's Joy:

_____

_____

_____

_____

_____

The best thing to happen during the past week

_____

_____

_____

Something yummy you ate

_____

_____

_____

A moment you wished would never end

_____

_____

_____

Today's Date: _____

This Day's Joy:

_____

_____

_____

_____

_____

Something funny that occurred recently

_____

_____

_____

A favorite memory of playing as a child

_____

_____

_____

Something unexpectedly wonderful that happened to you

_____

_____

_____

Today's Date: _____

This Day's Joy:

_____

_____

_____

_____

_____

A change of scene you enjoy

_____

_____

_____

Added to or crossed off your bucket list

_____

_____

_____

Someone you'd love to talk to...and why

_____

_____

_____

Today's Date: _____

This Day's Joy:

_____

_____

_____

_____

_____

Something that made you happy today

_____

_____

_____

A way you like to raise your heart rate

_____

_____

_____

A guilty pleasure

_____

_____

_____

Today's Date: _____

This Day's Joy:

_____

_____

_____

_____

_____

Something nice someone said to you

_____

_____

_____

The best part of waking up on a weekend day

_____

_____

_____

Something you'd like to try that you've never done before

_____

_____

_____

Today's Date: _____

This Day's Joy:

_____

_____

_____

_____

_____

A scrumptious snack

_____

_____

_____

If you could turn back time — one of your best days ever

_____

_____

_____

An act of generosity — given or received

_____

_____

_____

Today's Date: _____

This Day's Joy:

_____

_____

_____

_____

_____

Five positive words to describe your day

_____

_____

_____

A sound you noticed that made you happy

_____

_____

_____

A gorgeous sight to behold

_____

_____

_____

Today's Date: _____

This Day's Joy:

_____

_____

_____

_____

_____

The best thing about you today

_____

_____

_____

A sport or activity you've always wanted to try...and why

_____

_____

_____

The best thing that happened during the past week

_____

_____

_____

Today's Date: _____

This Day's Joy:

_____

_____

_____

_____

_____

A few of your favorites things

_____

_____

_____

A reason to look forward to next week

_____

_____

_____

Something new you tried and failed at...gloriously

_____

_____

_____

Today's Date: _____

This Day's Joy:

_____

_____

_____

_____

_____

A small triumph you achieved

_____

_____

_____

A sign of the changing seasons that you like

_____

_____

_____

A positive reframe – a time you chose a better focus

_____

_____

_____

Today's Date: _____

This Day's Joy:

_____

_____

_____

_____

_____

A quotation that inspires you

_____

_____

_____

One reason you wouldn't trade places with anyone else

_____

_____

_____

A happy surprise – no matter how small

_____

_____

_____

Today's Date: _____

This Day's Joy:

_____

_____

_____

_____

_____

An attitude change that made all the difference

_____

_____

_____

A personal luxury — something just for you

_____

_____

_____

Describe a memorable moment from the last month

_____

_____

_____

Today's Date: _____

This Day's Joy:

_____

_____

_____

_____

_____

A game you enjoy playing

_____

_____

_____

An averted disaster — you're lucky to be alive

_____

_____

_____

A compliment you received

_____

_____

_____

Today's Date: _____

This Day's Joy:

_____

_____

_____

_____

_____

The best thing you smelled today

_____

_____

_____

Something that never fails to brighten your day

_____

_____

_____

Childhood fantasties — something you thought about as a kid

_____

_____

_____

Today's Date: _____

This Day's Joy:

_____

_____

_____

_____

_____

A favorite holiday

_____

_____

_____

Something that made you smile

_____

_____

_____

The best thing that happened during the past week

_____

_____

_____

Today's Date: _____

This Day's Joy:

_____

_____

_____

_____

_____

A random act of kindness done for someone else

_____

_____

_____

Something that always relaxes you

_____

_____

_____

A tasty treat for dessert

_____

_____

_____

Today's Date: _____

This Day's Joy:

_____

_____

_____

_____

_____

A reason you admire someone famous

_____

_____

_____

Something that made you laugh

_____

_____

_____

A good thought to go to sleep on

_____

_____

_____

Today's Date: _____

This Day's Joy:

_____

_____

_____

_____

_____

Three positive words to describe this day

_____

_____

_____

Your all-time favorite movie...and why

_____

_____

_____

A weight off your shoulders

_____

_____

_____

Today's Date: _____

This Day's Joy:

_____

_____

_____

_____

_____

Something that makes you feel cozy and safe

_____

_____

_____

A reason to look forward to next week

_____

_____

_____

Something you notice in peaceful moments

_____

_____

_____

Today's Date: _____

This Day's Joy:

_____

_____

_____

_____

_____

Paint a word picture of something lovely outdoors

_____

_____

_____

A small victory you achieved today

_____

_____

_____

A few of your favorites things

_____

_____

_____

Today's Date: _____

This Day's Joy:

_____

_____

_____

_____

_____

A book to add to your "must read" list

_____

_____

_____

A day you wished would last longer

_____

_____

_____

Something tasty you ate for dinner

_____

_____

_____

Today's Date: _____

This Day's Joy:

_____

_____

_____

_____

_____

Something you fretted about that didn't happen

_____

_____

_____

A happy surprise you experienced years ago

_____

_____

_____

The best thing that happened during the past week

_____

_____

_____

Today's Date: _____

This Day's Joy:

_____
_____
_____
_____
_____

Something that made you happy today

_____
_____
_____

Describe an event worth remembering

_____
_____
_____

A fun time you had with friends

_____
_____
_____

Today's Date: _____

This Day's Joy:

_____

_____

_____

_____

_____

Added to or crossed off your bucket list

_____

_____

_____

A song that always brightens your mood

_____

_____

_____

A way you restore balance when you feel out of sorts

_____

_____

_____

Today's Date: _____

This Day's Joy:

_____

_____

_____

_____

_____

A favorite way to spend an afternoon off

_____

_____

_____

A personal luxury you'd enjoy right now

_____

_____

_____

The best part of waking up today

_____

_____

_____

Today's Date: _____

This Day's Joy:

_____

_____

_____

_____

_____

If you could turn back time — a best day ever

_____

_____

_____

One of your favorite ways to indulge yourself

_____

_____

_____

Your favorite thing to do on a sunny day

_____

_____

_____

Today's Date: _____

This Day's Joy:

_____

_____

_____

_____

_____

Something beautiful you heard

_____

_____

_____

A gorgeous sight to behold

_____

_____

_____

A treasure that's worth nothing...but is still priceless to you

_____

_____

_____

Today's Date: _____

This Day's Joy:

_____

_____

_____

_____

_____

An idea that intrigues you

_____

_____

_____

A bit of wonderfulness from nature

_____

_____

_____

The best thing about you today

_____

_____

_____

Today's Date: _____

This Day's Joy:

_____

_____

_____

_____

_____

Something you're looking forward to next week

_____

_____

_____

A smell that makes your nose happy

_____

_____

_____

The best thing about your current job

_____

_____

_____

Today's Date: _____

This Day's Joy:

_____

_____

_____

_____

_____

A physical activity or hobby you enjoyed during childhood

_____

_____

_____

Three positive words to describe this day

_____

_____

_____

A positive reframe — choosing a better focus

_____

_____

_____

Today's Date: _____

This Day's Joy:

_____

_____

_____

_____

_____

Best advice you'd like to give your thirteen-year-old self

_____

_____

_____

A funny thing that happened while driving

_____

_____

_____

A good reward at the end of the day

_____

_____

_____

Today's Date: _____

This Day's Joy:

_____

_____

_____

_____

_____

Something that rejuvenates you

_____

_____

_____

Describe your best shoes ever

_____

_____

_____

The best part of being with friends or family

_____

_____

_____

Today's Date: _____

This Day's Joy:

_____

_____

_____

_____

_____

A favorite memory from summertime

_____

_____

_____

A fragrance that had you inhaling

_____

_____

_____

Something that felt good

_____

_____

_____

Today's Date: _____

This Day's Joy:

_____

_____

_____

_____

_____

Someone you'd love to talk to again

_____

_____

_____

A memorable experience you had as a teenager

_____

_____

_____

Something kind someone said to you

_____

_____

_____

Today's Date: _____

This Day's Joy:

_____

_____

_____

_____

_____

A song you really love

_____

_____

_____

Something that made you feel contented

_____

_____

_____

A quotation that inspires you

_____

_____

_____

Today's Date: _____

This Day's Joy:

_____

_____

_____

_____

_____

An act of generosity – you giving to someone you love

_____

_____

_____

Your favorite lunch

_____

_____

_____

The best thing to happen during the past week

_____

_____

_____

Today's Date: _____

This Day's Joy:

_____

_____

_____

_____

_____

How did you feel the last time you gave someone a compliment

_____

_____

_____

If you could be anywhere on earth, where would you be

_____

_____

_____

A good thought to go to sleep on

_____

_____

_____

Today's Date: _____

This Day's Joy:

_____

_____

_____

_____

_____

Something silly that never fails to make you laugh

_____

_____

_____

A huge relief you experienced recently

_____

_____

_____

Something you're looking forward to next month

_____

_____

_____

Today's Date: _____

This Day's Joy:

_____

_____

_____

_____

_____

Your favorite place to be when you do nothing at all

_____

_____

_____

Something new you learned to do

_____

_____

_____

A reason you're glad to be alive

_____

_____

_____

Today's Date: _____

This Day's Joy:

_____

_____

_____

_____

_____

Your favorite thing about this time of year

_____

_____

_____

Paint a word picture of something lovely

_____

_____

_____

A way to show yourself a little bit of grace

_____

_____

_____

Today's Date: _____

This Day's Joy:

_____
_____
_____
_____
_____

Your favorite healthy snack

_____
_____
_____

A small victory while out shopping

_____
_____
_____

One positive word to describe your day

_____
_____
_____

Today's Date: _____

This Day's Joy:

_____
_____
_____
_____
_____

A bad habit that you eventually broke

_____
_____
_____

The best part of waking up today

_____
_____
_____

A natural wonder you'd love to visit someday

_____
_____
_____

Today's Date: _____

This Day's Joy:

_____
_____
_____
_____
_____

A reason you wouldn't trade places with anyone

_____
_____
_____

The best thing that happened during the past week

_____
_____
_____

Celebrate yourself - something weird you absolutely adore

_____
_____
_____

Today's Date: _____

This Day's Joy:

_____

_____

_____

_____

_____

A personal luxury

_____

_____

_____

Something you dreamed of becoming when you grew up

_____

_____

_____

A positive reframe — how could it have been much worse

_____

_____

_____

Today's Date: _____

This Day's Joy:

_____

_____

_____

_____

_____

A few of your favorites people

_____

_____

_____

A favorite winter holiday memory

_____

_____

_____

A way you surprised yourself

_____

_____

_____

Today's Date: _____

This Day's Joy:

_____

_____

_____

_____

_____

If you could turn back time — one of your best days ever

_____

_____

_____

A secret you'd love to share with someone

_____

_____

_____

Your favorite color

_____

_____

_____

Today's Date: _____

This Day's Joy:

_____

_____

_____

_____

_____

Something noticable only in quiet moments

_____

_____

_____

What's your favorite kind of music...and why

_____

_____

_____

A television show or movie that never fails to amuse

_____

_____

_____

Today's Date: _____

This Day's Joy:

_____
_____
_____
_____
_____

A happy surprise in the last month

_____
_____
_____

A time you couldn't believe your eyes

_____
_____
_____

Something you're looking forward to next year

_____
_____
_____

Today's Date: _____

This Day's Joy:

_____

_____

_____

_____

_____

Something that always feels good to do

_____

_____

_____

The best thing about you today

_____

_____

_____

Someone you admire

_____

_____

_____

Today's Date: _____

This Day's Joy:

_____

_____

_____

_____

_____

A fun time with friends from long ago

_____

_____

_____

Something nice someone said to you

_____

_____

_____

The best thing that happened during the past month

_____

_____

_____

Today's Date: _____

This Day's Joy:

_____

_____

_____

_____

_____

A positive reframe — choosing a better focus

_____

_____

_____

Your favorite thing abouty our favorite wild animal

_____

_____

_____

A goal you worked toward and achieved

_____

_____

_____

Today's Date: _____

This Day's Joy:

_____

_____

_____

_____

_____

If you could vacation anywhere on earth, where would you go

_____

_____

_____

An amazing taste

_____

_____

_____

Something you fretted about that didn't happen

_____

_____

_____

Today's Date: _____

This Day's Joy:

_____

_____

_____

_____

_____

A funny thing that happened to you recently

_____

_____

_____

Something you wish you'd known at age thirteen

_____

_____

_____

Three positive words to describe your day

_____

_____

_____

Today's Date: _____

This Day's Joy:

_____

_____

_____

_____

_____

The song you'd hope was playing if you turned on the radio

_____

_____

_____

Something that made you happy when you were five-years-old

_____

_____

_____

Your favorite drink when you're hot and tired

_____

_____

_____

Today's Date: _____

This Day's Joy:

_____
_____
_____
_____
_____

A fist pump moment you'd love to relive

_____
_____
_____

A connection with nature that relaxed you

_____
_____
_____

Childhood memories — a favorite friend from the playground

_____
_____
_____

Today's Date: _____

This Day's Joy:

_____

_____

_____

_____

_____

What's in your life that you wouldn't trade for anything

_____

_____

_____

Best thing about your current living space

_____

_____

_____

An unexpected positive that made you happy

_____

_____

_____

Today's Date: _____

This Day's Joy:

_____

_____

_____

_____

_____

The best thing that happened during the last couple of weeks

_____

_____

_____

Describe a time you felt strong and capable

_____

_____

_____

A good thought to go to sleep on

_____

_____

_____

Today's Date: _____

This Day's Joy:

_____

_____

_____

_____

_____

A weight off your shoulders

_____

_____

_____

Something beautiful you encountered

_____

_____

_____

Your favorite technological gadget or gizmo

_____

_____

_____

Today's Date: _____

This Day's Joy:

_____
_____
_____
_____
_____

Something creative you did today

_____
_____
_____

Something you're looking forward to doing years from now

_____
_____
_____

An inspirational quotation

_____
_____
_____

Today's Date: _____

This Day's Joy:

_____

_____

_____

_____

_____

What's the best thing about your favorite musical instrument

_____

_____

_____

A compliment – given or received

_____

_____

_____

Paint a word picture of something lovely

_____

_____

_____

Today's Date: _____

This Day's Joy:

_____

_____

_____

_____

_____

Dream big! Describe your dream vehicle

_____

_____

_____

An unwritten rule you ignored recently

_____

_____

_____

A way you helped someone today

_____

_____

_____

Today's Date: _____

This Day's Joy:

_____

_____

_____

_____

_____

An aspect of nature you always marvel at

_____

_____

_____

The best part of waking up this morning

_____

_____

_____

A color you love to wear or enjoy in your surroundings

_____

_____

_____

Today's Date: _____

This Day's Joy:

_____

_____

_____

_____

_____

The best part of being out and about

_____

_____

_____

A personal luxury — something just for you

_____

_____

_____

An act of generosity you experienced

_____

_____

_____

Today's Date: _____

This Day's Joy:

_____

_____

_____

_____

_____

The best part of staying indoors

_____

_____

_____

The best thing that happened during the past week

_____

_____

_____

Three positive words to describe this day

_____

_____

_____

Today's Date: _____

This Day's Joy:

_____

_____

_____

_____

_____

A "should have" or "oughtta" you rejected

_____

_____

_____

Someone you'd love to talk to today

_____

_____

_____

A good reason to do a happy dance

_____

_____

_____

Today's Date: _____

This Day's Joy:

_____

_____

_____

_____

_____

A song that fits your mood today

_____

_____

_____

Something that felt good to say out loud

_____

_____

_____

How you felt the last time you tried something new

_____

_____

_____

Today's Date: _____

This Day's Joy:

_____

_____

_____

_____

_____

Something silly that never fails to make you laugh

_____

_____

_____

If you could be anywhere on earth, where would you be

_____

_____

_____

A totally unexpected, but happy surprise

_____

_____

_____

Today's Date: _____

This Day's Joy:

_____

_____

_____

_____

_____

A sound you love to hear

_____

_____

_____

If you could turn back time — a favorite outdoor game

_____

_____

_____

A beautiful sight - underwater

_____

_____

_____

Today's Date: _____

This Day's Joy:

_____

_____

_____

_____

_____

A magazine or journal you look forward to reading

_____

_____

_____

Something you're eagerly anticipating in the coming days

_____

_____

_____

Something kind someone said to you

_____

_____

_____

168

Today's Date: _____

This Day's Joy:

_____

_____

_____

_____

_____

The best thing about you today

_____

_____

_____

A sneaky indulgence

_____

_____

_____

A sign of the changing seasons that you love

_____

_____

_____

Today's Date: _____

This Day's Joy:

_____

_____

_____

_____

_____

The best thing that happened during the past week

_____

_____

_____

A positive reframe — the best thing about your dentist

_____

_____

_____

A memorable time you spent with family

_____

_____

_____

Today's Date: _____

This Day's Joy:

_____

_____

_____

_____

_____

A practical joke you pulled off successfully

_____

_____

_____

A reason you're glad to be alive

_____

_____

_____

A hobby that you'd like to spend more time doing

_____

_____

_____

Today's Date: _____

This Day's Joy:

_____

_____

_____

_____

_____

Something that makes you happy

_____

_____

_____

Your favorite place to take an afternoon walk

_____

_____

_____

A reason you're fiercely glad you're you

_____

_____

_____

Today's Date: _____

This Day's Joy:

_____

_____

_____

_____

_____

Your best advice to your seventy-year-old self

_____

_____

_____

A way you were spontaneous today

_____

_____

_____

If you had an unlimited budget, where would you go shopping

_____

_____

_____

Today's Date: _____

This Day's Joy:

_____

_____

_____

_____

_____

Something that made you laugh today

_____

_____

_____

If you could spend the day with someone, who would it be

_____

_____

_____

Three positive words to describe this day

_____

_____

_____

Today's Date: _____

This Day's Joy:

_____

_____

_____

_____

_____

Something noticable in a quiet moment

_____

_____

_____

A positive reframe — a dark cloud with a silver lining

_____

_____

_____

A favorite springtime holiday memory

_____

_____

_____

Today's Date: _____

This Day's Joy:

_____

_____

_____

_____

_____

Something you dreamed about doing as a kid

_____

_____

_____

A connection with nature

_____

_____

_____

A good thought to go to sleep on

_____

_____

_____

Today's Date: _____

This Day's Joy:

_____

_____

_____

_____

_____

There's a knock at the door. Who do you hope is on the other side

_____

_____

_____

The best thing that happened during the past week

_____

_____

_____

The best reason to give a huge sigh of relief

_____

_____

_____

Today's Date: _____

This Day's Joy:

_____

_____

_____

_____

_____

Paint a word picture of your favorite place

_____

_____

_____

A childhood obsession you're totally over

_____

_____

_____

An activity that always brightens your mood

_____

_____

_____

Finding This Day's Joy

Today's Date: _____

This Day's Joy:

_____

_____

_____

_____

_____

Something you're looking forward to next week

_____

_____

_____

A fun time you had going out with friends

_____

_____

_____

A few of your favorites places

_____

_____

_____

Today's Date: _____

This Day's Joy:

_____

_____

_____

_____

_____

A compliment – given or received

_____

_____

_____

Something you adore about a furry, feathered, or finny friend

_____

_____

_____

Something tasty you ate for breakfast, lunch, or dinner today

_____

_____

_____

Today's Date: _____

This Day's Joy:

_____

_____

_____

_____

_____

A personal luxury — something just for you

_____

_____

_____

Something that felt good to NOT do

_____

_____

_____

Something you did that's fun or funny only in retrospect

_____

_____

_____

Today's Date: _____

This Day's Joy:

_____

_____

_____

_____

_____

Something beautiful you encountered

_____

_____

_____

The best part of waking up this week

_____

_____

_____

An inspirational thought or quotation

_____

_____

_____

Today's Date: _____

This Day's Joy:

_____

_____

_____

_____

_____

The best aspect of your regular daily routine

_____

_____

_____

A way you nurture and care for yourself

_____

_____

_____

A memorable late-night adventure

_____

_____

_____

Today's Date: _____

This Day's Joy:

_____

_____

_____

_____

_____

Something nice someone said to you

_____

_____

_____

A favorite from your personal Top 10 playlist

_____

_____

_____

The best thing that happened during the past week

_____

_____

_____

Today's Date: _____

This Day's Joy:

_____

_____

_____

_____

_____

Something you'd like to add to your bucket list

_____

_____

_____

Something you worried about that didn't happen

_____

_____

_____

Your favorite things about your favorite season of the year

_____

_____

_____

Today's Date: _____

This Day's Joy:

_____

_____

_____

_____

_____

A physical activity you enjoy

_____

_____

_____

Something you wouldn't trade for all the money in the world

_____

_____

_____

One positive word to describe this day

_____

_____

_____

Today's Date: _____

This Day's Joy:

_____

_____

_____

_____

_____

A gorgeous sight to behold

_____

_____

_____

The very best way to end a long week

_____

_____

_____

Something that made you happy way back in the day

_____

_____

_____

Today's Date: _____

This Day's Joy:

_____

_____

_____

_____

_____

If you could turn back time — a best early morning ever

_____

_____

_____

Something you're looking forward to next week

_____

_____

_____

A weirdly wonderful fact about you

_____

_____

_____

Finding This Day's Joy

Today's Date: _____

This Day's Joy:

_____

_____

_____

_____

_____

A reason to stand up and cheer

_____

_____

_____

A way you expressed your creativity today

_____

_____

_____

Something funny that happened last week

_____

_____

_____

Today's Date: _____

This Day's Joy:

_____

_____

_____

_____

_____

A positive reframe — choosing a better focus

_____

_____

_____

The best thing about you today

_____

_____

_____

A few of your favorites things

_____

_____

_____

Today's Date: _____

This Day's Joy:

_____

_____

_____

_____

_____

The most exhilarating thing that happened this week

_____

_____

_____

Make a list of words that are fun to say aloud

_____

_____

_____

Good news you'd love to share with someone

_____

_____

_____

Today's Date: _____

This Day's Joy:

_____

_____

_____

_____

_____

The best part of going to bed tonight

_____

_____

_____

You've hit channel surfing gold...what's on the television

_____

_____

_____

An act of generosity that benefitted you

_____

_____

_____

Today's Date: _____

This Day's Joy:

_____

_____

_____

_____

_____

If you could be anywhere on earth, you'd be....

_____

_____

_____

The best part of being outside today

_____

_____

_____

Something that felt good to say aloud

_____

_____

_____

Today's Date: _____

This Day's Joy:

_____

_____

_____

_____

_____

Someone you'd love to talk to

_____

_____

_____

A book you'd like to dive into

_____

_____

_____

The sprinkles on the cupcake of your life

_____

_____

_____

Today's Date: _____

This Day's Joy:

_____
_____
_____
_____
_____

The best things in life are free...and...GO!

_____
_____
_____

A good reason to turn up your radio

_____
_____
_____

A good thought to go to sleep on for first thing tomorrow

_____
_____
_____

Today's Date: _____

This Day's Joy:

_____

_____

_____

_____

_____

Paint a word picture of something beautiful

_____

_____

_____

Something silly you always laugh at

_____

_____

_____

A good habit you have

_____

_____

_____

Today's Date: _____

This Day's Joy:

_____
_____
_____
_____
_____

Your favorite kind of candy to get on Halloween

_____
_____
_____

A weight off your shoulders

_____
_____
_____

Three positive words to describe this day

_____
_____
_____

Today's Date: _____

This Day's Joy:

_____

_____

_____

_____

_____

Something to crow about

_____

_____

_____

Something kind someone said to you

_____

_____

_____

The best thing that happened during the past week

_____

_____

_____

Today's Date: _____

This Day's Joy:

_____

_____

_____

_____

_____

Your best advice to your five-year-old self

_____

_____

_____

Something you're looking forward to next month

_____

_____

_____

A way to show yourself empathy

_____

_____

_____

Today's Date: _____

This Day's Joy:

_____
_____
_____
_____
_____

A thrilling memory of success

_____
_____
_____

A compliment – given or received

_____
_____
_____

Something delicious you ate today

_____
_____
_____

Today's Date: _____

This Day's Joy:

_____

_____

_____

_____

_____

Something that makes the "things I'm most thankful for" list

_____

_____

_____

The best reason you found to smile today

_____

_____

_____

Someone hands you a glass...what do you hope is inside

_____

_____

_____

201

Today's Date: _____

This Day's Joy:

_____
_____
_____
_____
_____

A positive reframe — lemons made into lemonade

_____
_____
_____

Your favorite web site to browse

_____
_____
_____

The best part of waking up before the alarm clock

_____
_____
_____

Today's Date: _____

This Day's Joy:

_____
_____
_____
_____
_____

A reason you wouldn't trade places with anyone today

_____
_____
_____

Something that made you laugh

_____
_____
_____

Describe your best "first date"

_____
_____
_____

Today's Date: _____

***This Day's Joy*:**

_____

_____

_____

_____

_____

Take a look back over the pages for something that stands out

_____

_____

_____

A quotation that inspires you to do better tomorrow

_____

_____

_____

A way you renew your spirit

_____

_____

_____

Today's Date: _____

This Day's Joy:

_____

_____

_____

_____

_____

A favorite summer holiday memory

_____

_____

_____

The best thing that happened during the past week

_____

_____

_____

A fun change of pace

_____

_____

_____

Today's Date: _____

This Day's Joy:

_____

_____

_____

_____

_____

Something you always become aware of when it's quiet

_____

_____

_____

A pleasant surprise from someone you love

_____

_____

_____

Something you've crossed off your to-do list this week

_____

_____

_____

Today's Date: _____

This Day's Joy:

_____
_____
_____
_____
_____

Childhood fantasties that have become realities

_____
_____
_____

A gorgeous sight to behold first thing in the morning

_____
_____
_____

A fun time with family

_____
_____
_____

Today's Date: _____

This Day's Joy:

_____

_____

_____

_____

_____

Three positive words to describe this day

_____

_____

_____

Something small that matters only to you

_____

_____

_____

A guilty pleasure you indulged in today

_____

_____

_____

Today's Date: _____

This Day's Joy:

_____

_____

_____

_____

_____

A stretch — mental or physical — that yielded good results

_____

_____

_____

Someone you admire who changed the way you see the world

_____

_____

_____

Turn back time to a day you learned to do something fun

_____

_____

_____

Today's Date: _____

This Day's Joy:

_____

_____

_____

_____

_____

A time a pet made you feel so much better

_____

_____

_____

A positive reframe — choosing a better focus

_____

_____

_____

The best thing about you today

_____

_____

_____

Today's Date: _____

This Day's Joy:

_____

_____

_____

_____

_____

Something to look forward to next year

_____

_____

_____

A fragrance that relaxes you

_____

_____

_____

A wonderful compliment — given or received

_____

_____

_____

Today's Date: _____

This Day's Joy:

_____

_____

_____

_____

_____

A dessert that leaves you licking the spoon

_____

_____

_____

Something nice someone said to you

_____

_____

_____

The best thing that happened during the past week

_____

_____

_____

Today's Date: _____

This Day's Joy:

_____
_____
_____
_____
_____

A way you were creative or innovative today

_____
_____
_____

A memory of a favorite childhood friend

_____
_____
_____

Your favorite real-world retail shop

_____
_____
_____

Today's Date: _____

This Day's Joy:

_____

_____

_____

_____

_____

A song that fits your mood at the moment

_____

_____

_____

Something you could do to make your life better...right now

_____

_____

_____

The quality you admire most in your best friend

_____

_____

_____

Today's Date: _____

This Day's Joy:

_____

_____

_____

_____

_____

Something you stewed about that didn't happen

_____

_____

_____

Describe your dream home

_____

_____

_____

A good thought to end the day with

_____

_____

_____

Today's Date: _____

This Day's Joy:

_____

_____

_____

_____

_____

Something you're looking forward to next month

_____

_____

_____

Something beautiful you saw in the mirror today

_____

_____

_____

The best thing about your life at this time in your life

_____

_____

_____

Today's Date: _____

This Day's Joy:

_____

_____

_____

_____

_____

A joyous surprise

_____

_____

A time in your life you absolutely did the right thing

_____

_____

_____

Four positive words to describe today

_____

_____

_____

Today's Date: _____

This Day's Joy:

_____

_____

_____

_____

_____

Paint a word picture of something lovely you saw today

_____

_____

_____

Your favorite "way back when" story your family tells

_____

_____

_____

A small personal victory you achieved recently

_____

_____

_____

Finding This Day's Joy

Today's Date: _____

This Day's Joy:

_____

_____

_____

_____

_____

A good news story that was in the news recently

_____

_____

_____

What do you like about your hair

_____

_____

_____

Something you're looking forward to next year

_____

_____

_____

Today's Date: _____

This Day's Joy:

_____

_____

_____

_____

_____

A quotation that inspires you

_____

_____

_____

Something tasty you ate for breakfast or lunch

_____

_____

_____

The best thing about late, late nights

_____

_____

_____

Today's Date: _____

This Day's Joy:

_____

_____

_____

_____

_____

The best part of waking up on a lazy day off

_____

_____

_____

Childhood playtime — what games did you love to play

_____

_____

_____

Salty or sweet — something you think is delicious

_____

_____

_____

221

Today's Date: _____

This Day's Joy:

_____

_____

_____

_____

_____

If you could be anywhere on earth, where would you be

_____

_____

_____

An act of generosity that benefitted you

_____

_____

_____

A happy sound you heard

_____

_____

_____

Finding This Day's Joy

Today's Date: _____

This Day's Joy:

_____

_____

_____

_____

_____

Something that makes you feel cozy and relaxed

_____

_____

_____

What made you smile today

_____

_____

_____

The best part of being outside at sunrise or sunset

_____

_____

_____

Today's Date: _____

This Day's Joy:

_____

_____

_____

_____

_____

Someone you'd love to spend the day with

_____

_____

_____

A soul soothing moment

_____

_____

_____

Something you've never done before that you'd like to try

_____

_____

_____

224

Today's Date: _____

This Day's Joy:

_____

_____

_____

_____

_____

Savoring a sign of the season – did you notice changes today

_____

_____

_____

Something that felt good to the touch

_____

_____

_____

A new recipe you'd like to make

_____

_____

_____

Today's Date: _____

This Day's Joy:

_____

_____

_____

_____

_____

Describe something memorable you've done alone

_____

_____

_____

Something silly that always make you laugh

_____

_____

_____

The best thing that happened during the past week

_____

_____

_____

Today's Date: _____

This Day's Joy:

_____

_____

_____

_____

_____

A good joke you've heard recently

_____

_____

_____

For you, what would be the best surprise imaginable

_____

_____

_____

The perfect view — what does it look like to you

_____

_____

_____

Today's Date: _____

This Day's Joy:

_____

_____

_____

_____

_____

Look back — what patterns do you see in what you've written

_____

_____

_____

A freebie you found

_____

_____

_____

A way to treat yourself right today

_____

_____

_____

Today's Date: _____

This Day's Joy:

_____

_____

_____

_____

_____

If you'd only known — best advice to your younger self

_____

_____

_____

Turn up the radio — a song you really love

_____

_____

_____

If you could turn back time — what would you tell your parents

_____

_____

_____

Today's Date: _____

This Day's Joy:

_____
_____
_____
_____
_____

The best thing about you today

_____
_____
_____

Three positive words to describe this year to date

_____
_____
_____

Something you're looking forward to next week

_____
_____
_____

Today's Date: _____

This Day's Joy:

_____

_____

_____

_____

_____

A tasty treat

_____

_____

_____

Something you value that's not "stuff"

_____

_____

_____

A teacher who made a difference in your life

_____

_____

_____

Today's Date: _____

This Day's Joy:

_____

_____

_____

_____

_____

A favorite dumb riddle that makes you laugh

_____

_____

_____

The best part of starting a new project

_____

_____

_____

A childhood friend you'd love to see again

_____

_____

_____

Finding This Day's Joy

Today's Date: _____

This Day's Joy:

_____
_____
_____
_____
_____

Something new you learned

_____
_____
_____

The best thing that happened during the past week

_____
_____
_____

Something that made you happy today

_____
_____
_____

Today's Date: _____

This Day's Joy:

_____

_____

_____

_____

_____

A favorite fall holiday memory

_____

_____

_____

Your favorite way to spend an evening alone

_____

_____

_____

A postive reframe – an attitude change that made a difference

_____

_____

_____

Today's Date: _____

This Day's Joy:

_____

_____

_____

_____

_____

Something added to or crossed off your bucket list

_____

_____

_____

A good thought to go to sleep on

_____

_____

_____

A way to show someone you care

_____

_____

_____

Today's Date: _____

This Day's Joy:

_____

_____

_____

_____

_____

A time you felt strong and capable

_____

_____

_____

Describe something worth remembering, and remembering well

_____

_____

_____

The best thing about total quiet

_____

_____

_____

Today's Date: _____

This Day's Joy:

_____

_____

_____

_____

_____

The best thing about finishing a long-term project

_____

_____

_____

A weight off your shoulders

_____

_____

_____

A fun surprise you'd like to plan for someone

_____

_____

_____

Today's Date: _____

This Day's Joy:

_____

_____

_____

_____

_____

A good reason to admire someone

_____

_____

_____

A few of your favorites things about being in the city

_____

_____

_____

A personal success story you're proud of

_____

_____

_____

Today's Date: _____

This Day's Joy:

_____

_____

_____

_____

_____

Your favorite place to window shop or browse

_____

_____

_____

Paint a word picture of something lovely

_____

_____

_____

Childhood fantasies — what did you dream about

_____

_____

_____

Today's Date: _____

This Day's Joy:

_____
_____
_____
_____
_____

Something yummy you ate today

_____
_____
_____

Something you're looking forward to next week

_____
_____
_____

The best thing that happened to you during the past week

_____
_____
_____

240

Today's Date: _____

This Day's Joy:

_____
_____
_____
_____
_____

One positive word that encapsulates your day

_____
_____
_____

The best part of waking up on a Monday morning

_____
_____
_____

Something that felt good to say or do

_____
_____
_____

Today's Date: _____

This Day's Joy:

_____

_____

_____

_____

_____

If size and money were not issues, what pet would you get

_____

_____

_____

Celebrate yourself — what do you love that other people don't

_____

_____

_____

Something beautiful you encountered while out shopping

_____

_____

_____

Today's Date: _____

This Day's Joy:

_____

_____

_____

_____

_____

Something that made you smile at a restaurant

_____

_____

_____

A positive reframe — choosing a better focus

_____

_____

_____

A pleasant surprise at the end of a long day

_____

_____

_____

Today's Date: _____

This Day's Joy:

_____

_____

_____

_____

_____

What's the best concert you've ever been to

_____

_____

_____

A way you can jump-start a day or week that started poorly

_____

_____

_____

A favorite school memory

_____

_____

_____

Today's Date: _____

This Day's Joy:

_____

_____

_____

_____

_____

Something nice someone said to you

_____

_____

_____

A moment that felt peaceful

_____

_____

_____

A quotation that inspires you

_____

_____

_____

Today's Date: _____

This Day's Joy:

_____

_____

_____

_____

_____

Something you worried about that turned out to be no big deal

_____

_____

_____

A breathtaking view you've never seen but would like to

_____

_____

_____

The perfect drink at the end of a long day

_____

_____

_____

Today's Date: _____

This Day's Joy:

_____

_____

_____

_____

_____

The best thing to happen during the past week

_____

_____

_____

A compliment – given or received

_____

_____

_____

Shhhh, don't tell – a sneaky indulgence

_____

_____

_____

Today's Date: _____

This Day's Joy:

_____

_____

_____

_____

_____

Something funny that happened recently

_____

_____

_____

Wouldn't trade it for all the money in the world

_____

_____

_____

Describe a happy, unforgettable moment you've experienced

_____

_____

_____

Today's Date: _____

This Day's Joy:

_____

_____

_____

_____

_____

If you could turn back time — your best Halloween costume

_____

_____

_____

Something creative you did today

_____

_____

_____

Review this journal – what have you learned so far

_____

_____

_____

Today's Date: _____

This Day's Joy:

_____

_____

_____

_____

_____

A "should have" that you totally rejected today

_____

_____

_____

If you could be anywhere on earth, you'd be....

_____

_____

_____

Something impressive you did today

_____

_____

_____

Today's Date: _____

This Day's Joy:

_____

_____

_____

_____

_____

A positive reframe — choosing a better focus

_____

_____

_____

Childhood memories — what made you happy way back when

_____

_____

_____

A fragrance that had you inhaling deeply

_____

_____

_____

Today's Date: _____

This Day's Joy:

_____

_____

_____

_____

_____

Something you're looking forward to next week

_____

_____

_____

The best part of being outside in nature

_____

_____

_____

Three positive words to describe your day

_____

_____

_____

Today's Date: _____

This Day's Joy:

_____

_____

_____

_____

_____

A new song you heard that you'd like to hear again

_____

_____

_____

Someone you'd love to talk to

_____

_____

_____

If you'd only known — best advice to your younger self

_____

_____

_____

Today's Date: _____

This Day's Joy:

_____

_____

_____

_____

_____

The best thing that happened during the past week

_____

_____

_____

Something you love about this particular time of year

_____

_____   _____

_____

Something that makes you happy about the current weather

_____

_____

_____

Today's Date: _____

This Day's Joy:

_____

_____

_____

_____

_____

A book that inspires you

_____

_____

_____

Something new you would like to experience

_____

_____

_____

A good thought to go to sleep on

_____

_____

_____

Today's Date: _____

This Day's Joy:

_____

_____

_____

_____

_____

The best personal reward for a job well done

_____

_____

_____

The best thing about your all time favorite movie

_____

_____

_____

Something that always makes you laugh

_____

_____

_____

Finding This Day's Joy

Today's Date: _____

This Day's Joy:

_____

_____

_____

_____

_____

Something it felt good to say NO to

_____

_____

_____

A person who influenced your life for the better

_____

_____

_____

A creative solution you discovered for a problem you've had

_____

_____

_____

Today's Date: _____

This Day's Joy:

_____

_____

_____

_____

_____

Your favorite way to pay it forward

_____

_____

_____

Someone you're especially thankful for

_____

_____

_____

The comfort foods you turn to in times of stress

_____

_____

_____

Today's Date: _____

This Day's Joy:

_____

_____

_____

_____

_____

A famous piece of artwork you'd love to have in your home

_____

_____

_____

Something kind someone said to you

_____

_____

_____

Talent Show – name a unique ability you have

_____

_____

_____

Today's Date: _____

This Day's Joy:

_____

_____

_____

_____

_____

A game you enjoy playing

_____

_____

_____

Your very best vacation destination

_____

_____

_____

Something that made you laugh today

_____

_____

_____

Today's Date: _____

This Day's Joy:

_____

_____

_____

_____

_____

Something you enjoy about your home space

_____

_____

_____

The reason you admire a famous person

_____

_____

_____

The best things to happen during this month

_____

_____

_____

Today's Date: _____

This Day's Joy:

_____

_____

_____

_____

_____

Something totally crazy that you did...and survived

_____

_____

_____

A fresh perspective that motivated you to shake things up

_____

_____

_____

A way you helped someone today

_____

_____

_____

Today's Date: _____

This Day's Joy:

_____

_____

_____

_____

_____

Something you're looking forward to next week

_____

_____

_____

The best part of waking up

_____

_____

_____

Three positive words to describe this day

_____

_____

_____

Today's Date: _____

This Day's Joy:

_____

_____

_____

_____

_____

A time joy leaked out your eyes and ran down your cheeks

_____

_____

_____

A fun time with friends

_____

_____

_____

Something soothing and relaxing for you

_____

_____

_____

Today's Date: _____

This Day's Joy:

_____

_____

_____

_____

_____

Something you'd like to add to your bucket list

_____

_____

_____

Something you love to smell baking

_____

_____

_____

A favorite winter holiday memory

_____

_____

_____

Today's Date: _____

This Day's Joy:

_____

_____

_____

_____

_____

A welcome sight first thing in the morning

_____

_____

_____

A positive reframe — one way it could have been worse

_____

_____

_____

A tasty treat at the end of a long week

_____

_____

_____

Today's Date: _____

This Day's Joy:

_____

_____

_____

_____

_____

Something you thought was lost forever that you found again

_____

_____

_____

If you could be anywhere else in the world, where would you be

_____

_____

_____

Describe your favorite friend or relative

_____

_____

_____

Today's Date: _____

This Day's Joy:

_____

_____

_____

_____

_____

Your favorite thing in your childhood bedroom

_____

_____

_____

The best thing that happened to you this past week

_____

_____

_____

A compliment you gave to someone...how did you feel afterwards

_____

_____

_____

Today's Date: _____

This Day's Joy:

_____

_____

_____

_____

_____

Best thing about a rainy day

_____

_____

_____

A tiny triumph on the homefront

_____

_____

_____

Mental vacation — a great place to visit...if only in your mind

_____

_____

_____

Today's Date: _____

This Day's Joy:

_____

_____

_____

_____

_____

A positive reframe — choosing a better focus

_____

_____

_____

Childhood fantasties — something exciting you dreamed of doing

_____

_____

_____

Describe your dream vacation

_____

_____

_____

Today's Date: _____

This Day's Joy:

_____

_____

_____

_____

_____

A person you've met that you admire

_____

_____

_____

The best thing about you today

_____

_____

_____

A way to show yourself empathy

_____

_____

_____

Today's Date: _____

This Day's Joy:

_____

_____

_____

_____

_____

A few of your favorites things

_____

_____

_____

Something that felt good to achieve...finally

_____

_____

_____

A great moment with a furry, finny, or feathered friend

_____

_____

_____

Today's Date: _____

This Day's Joy:

_____

_____

_____

_____

_____

The perfect bedtime snack

_____

_____

_____

A favorite childhood memory of riding in a car

_____

_____

_____

Which superpower would you love to possess

_____

_____

_____

Today's Date: _____

This Day's Joy:

_____

_____

_____

_____

_____

Something funny that happened

_____

_____

_____

Three positive words to describe this day

_____

_____

_____

Your favorite song when you were eight-years-old

_____

_____

_____

Today's Date: _____

This Day's Joy:

_____
_____
_____
_____
_____

The best thing that happened during the past week

_____
_____
_____

A good thought right at bedtime

_____
_____
_____

Something that brings you a sense of peace and contentment

_____
_____
_____

Today's Date: _____

This Day's Joy:

_____

_____

_____

_____

_____

Something noticable in quiet times

_____

_____

_____

Your best walk — is it forest, mountains, beach or prairie

_____

_____

_____

Something kind that someone said to you

_____

_____

_____

Finding This Day's Joy

Today's Date: _____

This Day's Joy:

_____

_____

_____

_____

_____

Something beautiful you saw

_____

_____

_____

A weight off your shoulders

_____

_____

_____

Something that made you laugh today

_____

_____

_____

Today's Date: _____

This Day's Joy:

_____

_____

_____

_____

_____

A song that takes you back in time

_____

_____

_____

An activity you wish you could do more often

_____

_____

_____

What's the most important thing in your life right now

_____

_____

_____

Today's Date: _____

This Day's Joy:

_____

_____

_____

_____

_____

The best part of being outside

_____

_____

_____

A special event you're looking forward to next year

_____

_____

_____

Something that always reminds you of home

_____

_____

_____

Today's Date: _____

This Day's Joy:

_____

_____

_____

_____

_____

An amazing fragrance that's only there during the summer

_____

_____

_____

Something you worried about that didn't happen

_____

_____

_____

If you could be anywhere on earth, where would you be

_____

_____

_____

Today's Date: _____

This Day's Joy:

_____

_____

_____

_____

_____

Childhood memories — what made you happy way back when

_____

_____

_____

A yummy snack you sneaked a bite of

_____

_____

_____

Your favorite big purchase — car, house, boat, jewelry, other

_____

_____

_____

Today's Date: _____

This Day's Joy:

_____

_____

_____

_____

_____

A glorious indulgence that you wish happened more often

_____

_____

_____

The best thing that happened during the past week

_____

_____

_____

Paint a word picture of something you enjoy doing

_____

_____

_____

Today's Date: _____

This Day's Joy:

_____

_____

_____

_____

_____

The best part of waking up on a sunny day

_____

_____

_____

A fun occasion you planned for someone

_____

_____

_____

Accomplishment you're most proud of

_____

_____

_____

Today's Date: _____

This Day's Joy:

_____

_____

_____

_____

_____

A peaceful moment

_____

_____

_____

A fun change of pace

_____

_____

_____

Think of eye candy – describe what you just imagined

_____

_____

_____

Today's Date: _____

This Day's Joy:

_____

_____

_____

_____

_____

Three positive words to describe your day

_____

_____

_____

An act of generosity you received

_____

_____

_____

A new food or drink you tried for the first time

_____

_____

_____

Today's Date: _____

This Day's Joy:

_____

_____

_____

_____

_____

Describe something you consider unforgettable

_____

_____

_____

Something that made you smile today

_____

_____

_____

Shhhh, don't tell — a sneaky indulgence

_____

_____

_____

Today's Date: _____

This Day's Joy:

_____

_____

_____

_____

_____

Someone you'd love to talk to today

_____

_____

_____

Something silly that never fails to make you giggle

_____

_____

_____

A happy sound you heard outside

_____

_____

_____

Today's Date: _____

This Day's Joy:

_____
_____
_____
_____
_____

Something that felt good to do or say

_____
_____
_____

Take a look back — whose name shows up most in this journal

_____
_____
_____

Savoring a sign of this time of year

_____
_____
_____

Finding This Day's Joy

Today's Date: _____

This Day's Joy:

_____

_____

_____

_____

_____

A food that always makes you want seconds

_____

_____

_____

A compliment you received recently

_____

_____

_____

The best thing that happened during the past month

_____

_____

_____

Today's Date: _____

This Day's Joy:

_____

_____

_____

_____

_____

A positive reframe – a dark cloud with a silver lining

_____

_____

_____

A thought that inspires you

_____

_____

_____

The best thing about you today

_____

_____

_____

Today's Date: _____

This Day's Joy:

_____

_____

_____

_____

_____

Something you're looking forward to next week

_____

_____

_____

A song that makes you want to sing along

_____

_____

_____

Something totally out of the blue that was terrific

_____

_____

_____

Today's Date: _____

This Day's Joy:

_____
_____
_____
_____
_____

A TV show you've seen every episode of...and more than once

_____
_____
_____

You did it! Name a tiny triumph from the last week

_____
_____
_____

A fun time you had with friends recently

_____
_____
_____

Today's Date: _____

This Day's Joy:

_____

_____

_____

_____

_____

A compliment — given or received — that made your day

_____

_____

_____

Why wouldn't you trade places with anyone else

_____

_____

_____

A connection with friends that makes you happy

_____

_____

_____

Today's Date: _____

This Day's Joy:

_____

_____

_____

_____

_____

Something that gladdens your heart each time it occurs

_____

_____

_____

Your favorite way to experience music

_____

_____

_____

A good thought to go to sleep on every day

_____

_____

_____

Today's Date: _____

This Day's Joy:

_____
_____
_____
_____
_____

Something you're eagerly anticipating doing next year

_____
_____
_____

Something that makes you giggle

_____
_____
_____

The most recent addition or cross-off from your bucket list

_____
_____
_____

Today's Date: _____

This Day's Joy:

_____

_____

_____

_____

_____

Describe your favorite thing to do on a snowy day

_____

_____

_____

A lovely spring holiday memory

_____

_____

_____

The best thing to happen to you during the past week

_____

_____

_____

Today's Date: _____

This Day's Joy:

_____

_____

_____

_____

_____

A problem you solved recently

_____

_____

_____

A date to circle on the calendar

_____

_____

_____

A huge relief

_____

_____

_____

Today's Date: _____

This Day's Joy:

_____

_____

_____

_____

_____

A good habit you are trying to cultivate

_____

_____

_____

The best thing you smelled today

_____

_____

_____

A book or movie character you'd like to spend the day with

_____

_____

_____

Finding This Day's Joy

Today's Date: _____

This Day's Joy:

_____

_____

_____

_____

_____

Something you're looking forward to next month

_____

_____

_____

A time you didn't give up on yourself and it paid off

_____

_____

_____

A favorite candy or salty snack you absolutely adore

_____

_____

_____

Today's Date: _____

This Day's Joy:

_____
_____
_____
_____
_____

Something tasty you ate today

_____
_____
_____

Something you're anticipating in the next few days

_____
_____
_____

Someone you've always respected...and why...

_____
_____
_____

Today's Date: _____

This Day's Joy:

_____

_____

_____

_____

_____

A positive reframe — choosing a better focus

_____

_____

_____

Someone you admire who is over sixty-years-old

_____

_____

_____

Something beautiful you encountered

_____

_____

_____

Today's Date: _____

This Day's Joy:

_____

_____

_____

_____

_____

Furry, feathered, or finny friends — a great pet moment

_____

_____

_____

Something that felt good to do for yourself

_____

_____

_____

A time you had the courage of your convictions

_____

_____

_____

Today's Date: _____

This Day's Joy:

_____

_____

_____

_____

_____

A welcome change in your regular routine

_____

_____

_____

Something that makes your heart melt

_____

_____

_____

The best thing that happened during the past week

_____

_____

_____

Today's Date: _____

This Day's Joy:

_____

_____

_____

_____

_____

The best part of waking up on a Friday morning

_____

_____

_____

Something that drives you "happy crazy"

_____

_____

_____

A relaxing way to spend an evening

_____

_____

_____

Today's Date: _____

This Day's Joy:

_____

_____

_____

_____

_____

Your favorite kitchen gadget ever

_____

_____

_____

Someone you admire who is less than twenty years old

_____

_____

_____

Something nice someone said to you

_____

_____

_____

Today's Date: _____

This Day's Joy:

_____

_____

_____

_____

_____

A time you asked for help and were grateful to receive it

_____

_____

_____

Paint a word picture of something you think is lovely

_____

_____

_____

You did it!! Something you've been working towards

_____

_____

_____

Today's Date: _____

This Day's Joy:

_____

_____

_____

_____

_____

If you could attend any concert this year, which one would it be

_____

_____

_____

The best advice you've ever gotten

_____

_____

_____

The best thing about quiet moments

_____

_____

_____

Today's Date: _____

This Day's Joy:

_____

_____

_____

_____

_____

Three positive words to describe this day

_____

_____

_____

Something that tastes like a sunny summer afternoon

_____

_____

_____

Turn back the clock — your best next door neighbor ever

_____

_____

_____

Finding This Day's Joy

Today's Date: _____

This Day's Joy:

_____

_____

_____

_____

_____

A little thing that makes life worth living

_____

_____

_____

A talent you have that you wish you could do more with

_____

_____

_____

What do you really really love about your phone or tablet

_____

_____

_____

Today's Date: _____

This Day's Joy:

_____

_____

_____

_____

_____

The best thing that happened during the past week

_____

_____

_____

Good news! The best world / national news right now

_____

___ _____

_____

Something you fretted about that didn't happen

_____

_____

_____

Today's Date: _____

This Day's Joy:

_____

_____

_____

_____

_____

The best thing about you today

_____

_____

_____

Something you're looking forward to doing when you're older

_____

_____

_____

A compliment you gave or received

_____

_____

_____

Today's Date: _____

This Day's Joy:

_____

_____

_____

_____

_____

The best part of being outside after dark

_____

_____

_____

Review this journal — give yourself advice on the third day

_____

_____

_____

If you could be anywhere on earth, where would you be

_____

_____

_____

Today's Date: _____

This Day's Joy:

_____

_____

_____

_____

_____

Something you would like to give away

_____

_____

_____

A way you'd enjoy relaxing tonight

_____

_____

_____

A quotation that inspires you

_____

_____

_____

Today's Date: _____

This Day's Joy:

_____

_____

_____

_____

_____

What made you happy ten years ago

_____

_____

_____

A bad habit you intentionally stopped

_____

_____

_____

A good thought at bedtime

_____

_____

_____

Today's Date: _____

This Day's Joy:

_____

_____

_____

_____

_____

A way you helped someone today

_____

_____

_____

Something new you learned in the last few days

_____

_____

_____

Make 'em laugh — who's your favorite funny person

_____

_____

_____

Today's Date: _____

This Day's Joy:

_____

_____

_____

_____

_____

Something you'd like to try

_____

_____

_____

A person you really appreciate on a regular basis

_____

_____

_____

If someone hands you a cup, what do you hope is inside

_____

_____

_____

Today's Date: _____

This Day's Joy:

_____
_____
_____
_____
_____

The best thing that happened during the past week

_____
_____
_____

A few of your favorites things

_____
_____
_____

Something that felt good to get off your chest

_____
_____
_____

Today's Date: _____

This Day's Joy:

_____

_____

_____

_____

_____

A weight off your shoulders

_____

_____

_____

Something you really appreciate about this time of year

_____

_____

_____

A routine, everyday task that gives you pleasure

_____

_____

_____

Today's Date: _____

This Day's Joy:

_____

_____

_____

_____

_____

Something you're looking forward to next year

_____

_____

_____

Favorite nickname of a friend or family member

_____

_____

_____

Three positive words to describe your day

_____

_____

_____

Today's Date: _____

This Day's Joy:

_____
_____
_____
_____
_____

A fun time you had with friends

_____
_____
_____

Someone from history you'd love to talk to

_____
_____
_____

A positive reframe — lemons into lemonade

_____
_____
_____

Today's Date: _____

This Day's Joy:

_____

_____

_____

_____

_____

FacePalm — a song lyric you can't believe you misunderstood

_____

_____

_____

A personal luxury — something just for me

_____

_____

_____

Something you'd love to do on your next 3-day weekend

_____

_____

_____

Today's Date: _____

This Day's Joy:

_____

_____

_____

_____

_____

The best scene from a movie...ever

_____

_____

_____

A kind word spoken to you

_____

_____

_____

A time you did something that surprised yourself

_____

_____

_____

Today's Date: _____

This Day's Joy:

_____

_____

_____

_____

_____

A book you enjoyed reading

_____

_____

_____

If you could be someone else for one day, who would you be

_____

_____

_____

A gift you always look forward to receiving

_____

_____

_____

Today's Date: _____

This Day's Joy:

_____

_____

_____

_____

_____

The best thing that happened during the past week

_____

_____

_____

Your favorite summer holiday memory

_____

_____   _____

_____

Something that made you smile today

_____

_____

_____

Today's Date: _____

This Day's Joy:

_____

_____

_____

_____

_____

It's your ultimate road trip — where are you headed

_____

_____

_____

The best compliment you've ever received

_____

_____

_____

Something that leaves you feeling cozy

_____

_____

_____

Today's Date: _____

This Day's Joy:

_____

_____

_____

_____

_____

Let's spend the day together — you and who...

_____

_____

_____

A small shopping triumph

_____

_____

_____

The best lazy morning breakfast you can imagine

_____

_____

_____

Today's Date: _____

This Day's Joy:

_____

_____

_____

_____

_____

A way you make a difference in the lives of those you love

_____

_____

_____

A thought that motivates you

_____

_____

_____

Something you did today to make for a better tomorrow

_____

_____

_____

Today's Date: _____

This Day's Joy:

_____
_____
_____
_____
_____

A few of your favorites things

_____
_____
_____

If you could turn back time — a best weekend ever

_____
_____
_____

Be good to yourself — how could you show yourself grace

_____
_____
_____

Finding This Day's Joy

Today's Date: _____

This Day's Joy:

_____
_____
_____
_____
_____

Three positive words to describe this day

_____
_____
_____

Something you're looking forward to next week

_____
_____
_____

Something funny you saw on television or read in a book

_____
_____
_____

Today's Date: _____

This Day's Joy:

_____

_____

_____

_____

_____

A way to make someone feel welcome

_____

_____

_____

Your go-to sneaky indulgence when no one is looking

_____

_____

_____

Furry, feathered, or finny friends — a great pet moment

_____

_____

_____

Today's Date: _____

This Day's Joy:

_____
_____
_____
_____
_____

The best thing that happened during the past week

_____
_____
_____

The best thing about you today

_____
_____
_____

A positive reframe — choosing a better focus

_____
_____
_____

Today's Date: _____

This Day's Joy:

_____
_____
_____
_____
_____

Castles in the air — your favorite daydream

_____
_____
_____

A connection you experienced with something from nature

_____
_____
_____

A silly social norm you sometimes choose to totally ignore

_____
_____
_____

Today's Date: _____

This Day's Joy:

_____

_____

_____

_____

_____

A fun hat you once wore

_____

_____

_____

Something beautiful you saw on your way home today

_____

_____

_____

A good thought to go to sleep on tonight

_____

_____

_____

Today's Date: _____

This Day's Joy:

_____

_____

_____

_____

_____

Something that makes you look forward to the future

_____

_____

_____

A movie that inspires you

_____

_____

_____

A goal you achieved after working toward it for a long time

_____

_____

_____

Today's Date: _____

This Day's Joy:

_____

_____

_____

_____

_____

Your best moment from the last year

_____

_____

_____

Something it felt good to say NO to

_____

_____

_____

A childhood memory of playing "let's pretend"

_____

_____

_____

Today's Date: _____

This Day's Joy:

_____

_____

_____

_____

_____

Something kind someone said to you

_____

_____

_____

Describe your favorite t-shirt

_____

_____

_____

Something goofy you dreamed about doing when you were a kid

_____

_____

_____

Today's Date: _____

This Day's Joy:

_____

_____

_____

_____

_____

A musical instrument that always puts you in a good mood

_____

_____

_____

A huge relief at a disaster you averted

_____

_____

_____

A comfort food you crave when things get rough

_____

_____

_____

Today's Date: _____

This Day's Joy:

_____

_____

_____

_____

_____

A surprise ending where everything turned out just right

_____

_____

_____

The best thing that happened during the past week

_____

_____

_____

A great way for you to unwind on a Friday night

_____

_____

_____

Today's Date: _____

This Day's Joy:

_____

_____

_____

_____

_____

Something you're looking forward to next week

_____

_____

_____

A triumph over modern technology

_____

_____

_____

Something yummy you ate last weekend

_____

_____

_____

Today's Date: _____

This Day's Joy:

_____
_____
_____
_____
_____

Three positive words to describe your day

_____
_____
_____

Something nice you can do for yourself that doesn't cost money

_____
_____
_____

A color you wish you could wear all the time

_____
_____
_____

Today's Date: _____

This Day's Joy:

_____

_____

_____

_____

_____

An event that totally exceeded your expectations

_____

_____

_____

Describe an unforgettable evening out with someone special

_____

_____

_____

Something you could gaze at forever

_____

_____

_____

Today's Date: _____

This Day's Joy:

_____
_____
_____
_____
_____

The best part of waking up this morning

_____
_____
_____

A time you knew you were being your authentic self

_____
_____
_____

Look back to last week — what do you wish you'd known then

_____
_____
_____

Today's Date: _____

This Day's Joy:

_____

_____

_____

_____

_____

What wouldn't you trade for all the money in the world

_____

_____

_____

Something you worried about that didn't happen

_____

_____

_____

A wonderful, but unexpected, gift you've received

_____

_____

_____

Today's Date: _____

This Day's Joy:

_____

_____

_____

_____

_____

A fragrance that had you breathing deeply

_____

_____

_____

Something that made you smile this morning

_____

_____

_____

A bumper sticker that made you laugh

_____

_____

_____

Today's Date: _____

This Day's Joy:

_____

_____

_____

_____

_____

The best thing that happened during the past week

_____

_____

_____

The ideal tasty treat at the end of a really long day

_____

_____

_____

Paint a word picture of a good time you had with family

_____

_____

_____

Today's Date: _____

This Day's Joy:

_____

_____

_____

_____

_____

Something new you've tried to learn recently

_____

_____

_____

A tiny bit of perfection

_____

_____

_____

Something that always amuses you

_____

_____

_____

346

Today's Date: _____

This Day's Joy:

_____
_____
_____
_____
_____

The best part of being outside early in the morning

_____
_____
_____

An act of generosity

_____
_____
_____

Describe your very best kind of day

_____
_____
_____

Today's Date: _____

This Day's Joy:

_____

_____

_____

_____

_____

A delicious flavor you try to make last as long as possible

_____

_____

_____

A time forgiveness made all the difference

_____

_____

_____

A good dream that really did come true

_____

_____

_____

Finding This Day's Joy

Today's Date: _____

This Day's Joy:

_____

_____

_____

_____

_____

A reason to be hopeful about the future

_____

_____

_____

Something you're looking forward to next week

_____

_____

_____

If you could turn back time — a vacation you'd like to live over

_____

_____

_____

Today's Date: _____

This Day's Joy:

_____

_____

_____

_____

_____

A song that makes you want to dance

_____

_____

_____

A fun time going out with friends this year

_____

_____

_____

Something that felt good to the touch

_____

_____

_____

Today's Date: _____

This Day's Joy:

_____

_____

_____

_____

_____

Someone you'd love to talk to right now

_____

_____

_____

A positive reframe — an attitude change that made a difference

_____

_____

_____

A way you encourage creativity in yourself

_____

_____

_____

Today's Date: _____

This Day's Joy:

_____
_____
_____
_____
_____

The best place for you to totally relax

_____
_____
_____

The best thing to happen to you during the past week

_____
_____
_____

Describe an unforgettable time with someone special to you

_____
_____
_____

_____

Finding This Day's Joy

Today's Date: _____

This Day's Joy:

_____

_____

_____

_____

_____

Three positive words to describe this day

_____

_____

_____

A cheerful sound

_____

_____

_____

Sweet dreams – three good thoughts to go to sleep on

_____

_____

_____

Today's Date: _____

This Day's Joy:

_____

_____

_____

_____

_____

A quotation that inspires you

_____

_____

_____

A favorite fall holiday memory

_____

_____

_____

Something that made you happy today

_____

_____

_____

Today's Date: _____

This Day's Joy:

_____

_____

_____

_____

_____

A kindness you shared with someone

_____

_____

_____

Something that's only funny in retrospect

_____

_____

_____

Which planet in the solar system would you visit if you could

_____

_____

_____

Today's Date: _____

This Day's Joy:

_____
_____
_____
_____
_____

A delicious smell to come home to

_____
_____
_____

Something you've added to or crossed off your bucket list

_____
_____
_____

A great party or celebration you've attended

_____
_____
_____

Finding This Day's Joy

Today's Date: _____

This Day's Joy:

_____

_____

_____

_____

_____

A way you can encourage someone you care about

_____

_____

_____

Something you're looking forward to next month

_____

_____

_____

A song that's especially meaningful to you at this time in your life

_____

_____

_____

357

Today's Date: _____

This Day's Joy:

_____
_____
_____
_____
_____

A weight off your shoulders

_____
_____
_____

Something kind or insightful someone said to you recently

_____
_____
_____

A good ending to an unhappy beginning

_____
_____
_____

Finding This Day's Joy

Today's Date: _____

This Day's Joy:

_____
_____
_____
_____
_____

Your go-to way to make your living space more beautiful

_____
_____
_____

Something inexpensive that seems quite luxurious

_____
_____
_____

The best thing that happened to you during the past week

_____
_____
_____

Today's Date: _____

This Day's Joy:

_____

_____

_____

_____

_____

Something that says "home" to you

_____

_____

_____

Your favorite view

_____

_____

_____

An unforgettable moment with your pet

_____

_____

_____

Today's Date: _____

This Day's Joy:

_____

_____

_____

_____

_____

Something you always look for when you go for a walk

_____

_____

_____

A way to let others know you appreciate them

_____

_____

_____

Something you love doing to relax

_____

_____

_____

Today's Date: _____

This Day's Joy:

_____

_____

_____

_____

_____

The best thing about your favorite restaurant in the world

_____

_____

_____

Something that felt good to say aloud

_____

_____

_____

A fun time with a friend you wish you could relive

_____

_____

_____

Today's Date: _____

This Day's Joy:

_____

_____

_____

_____

_____

A quality you don't have but would like to cultivate in yourself

_____

_____

_____

Something you do when you want to completely unplug

_____

_____

_____

The best thing about you today

_____

_____

_____

Today's Date: _____

This Day's Joy:

_____

_____

_____

_____

_____

A positive reframe — choosing a better focus

_____

_____

_____

Describe your most unforgettable vacation

_____

_____

_____

A way yoy can clear you head and gain new perspective

_____

_____

_____

Today's Date: _____

This Day's Joy:

_____

_____

_____

_____

_____

Something that made you smile today

_____

_____

_____

A teacher who made a big difference in your life

_____

_____

_____

Three positive words to describe this day

_____

_____

_____

Today's Date: _____

This Day's Joy:

_____

_____

_____

_____

_____

The best thing that happened during the past week

_____

_____

_____

Review this journal — which words have you used most

_____

_____

_____

Paint a word picture of someone you know and admire

_____

_____

_____

Today's Date: _____

This Day's Joy:

_____

_____

_____

_____

_____

A way to end your day on a positive note

_____

_____

_____

A small personal success

_____

_____

_____

A hobby you enjoy that encourages you to be creative

_____

_____

_____

Today's Date: _____

This Day's Joy:

_____

_____

_____

_____

_____

Childhood fantasties — something you dreamed about

_____

_____

_____

Something you're looking forward to next week

_____

_____

_____

A happy surprise you wish would happen again

_____

_____

_____

Today's Date: _____

This Day's Joy:

_____

_____

_____

_____

_____

The last time you cried happy tears

_____

_____

_____

Something you notice when you sit quietly for a while

_____

_____

_____

A favorite wintertime treat

_____

_____

_____

Today's Date: _____

This Day's Joy:

_____

_____

_____

_____

_____

Someone you'd love to talk to that you haven't seen in ages

_____

_____

_____

If you could turn back time — a best holiday ever

_____

_____

_____

The best thing you smelled in the kitchen

_____

_____

_____

Today's Date: _____

This Day's Joy:

_____

_____

_____

_____

_____

Something beautiful you found in your closet

_____

_____

_____

Childhood memories — what made you happy way back when

_____

_____

_____

The last time you wanted to give yourself a high five

_____

_____

_____

Today's Date: _____

This Day's Joy:

_____
_____
_____
_____
_____

A luxury you'd love to splurge on someday

_____
_____
_____

Something you're always happy to do

_____
_____
_____

Your favorite crayon in the big yellow box

_____
_____
_____

Today's Date: _____

This Day's Joy:

_____

_____

_____

_____

_____

A good thought for the first day of vacation

_____

_____

_____

Something kind someone said to you

_____

_____

_____

The best thing that happened during the past week

_____

_____

_____

Today's Date: _____

This Day's Joy:

_____

_____

_____

_____

_____

A special place you like to visit on a regular vasis

_____

_____

_____

Something free that you'd love to do this weekend

_____

_____

_____

A skill or hobby that you'd like to get better at

_____

_____

_____

Today's Date: _____

This Day's Joy:

_____

_____

_____

_____

_____

A compliment – given or received

_____

_____

_____

Three positive words to describe your day

_____

_____

_____

A favorite autumn holiday memory

_____

_____

_____

Today's Date: _____

This Day's Joy:

_____

_____

_____

_____

_____

A terrific surprise on the home front

_____

_____

_____

Your favorite thing about this time of year

_____

_____

_____

Do over!!! A fresh start you'd like to make

_____

_____

_____

Today's Date: _____

This Day's Joy:

_____

_____

_____

_____

_____

An act of generosity that affected you positively

_____

_____

_____

A small everyday success story for you

_____

_____

_____

A habit you have broken that you're thrilled is gone

_____

_____

_____

Today's Date: _____

This Day's Joy:

_____

_____

_____

_____

_____

A life goal you had when you were young that you've achieved

_____

_____

_____

A way you were creative today

_____

_____

_____

A large task you finished recently

_____

_____

_____

Today's Date: _____

This Day's Joy:

_____

_____

_____

_____

_____

Something you're looking forward to next year

_____

_____

_____

Your favorite thing to gnosh on when you're hungry

_____

_____

_____

A time you did something way outside your comfort zone

_____

_____

_____

Today's Date: _____

This Day's Joy:

_____
_____
_____
_____
_____

A sound that cheers you up

_____
_____
_____

A good reason to get out of bed in the morning

_____
_____
_____

The best thing that happened during the past week

_____
_____
_____

Today's Date: _____

This Day's Joy:

_____

_____

_____

_____

_____

A gift you'd like to give someone

_____

_____

_____

Something that makes you unique

_____

_____

_____

A hidden truth about yourself that you'd like to reveal to everyone

_____

_____

_____

Today's Date: _____

This Day's Joy:

_____

_____

_____

_____

_____

Looking back — a time this year you've consciously chosen joy

_____

_____

_____

Looking back — a truth about yourself you've accepted this year

_____

_____

_____

Looking back — a way you've grown as a person this year

_____

_____

_____

About the Author

Gina Prosch grew up in central Missouri, before taking off for college in Nebraska and Wyoming. She taught literature and writing at a small liberal arts college in South Carolina, before she sucummed to the lure of entrepreneurship.

Currently, she and her family— husband Richard and son Wyatt— live in Missouri in the house her grandparents built. In her off hours, she enjoys poking through antique shops, gardening, and hand piecing and quilting. She desperately wants to adopt a basset hound puppy.

Gina enjoys hearing from her readers, so please reach out through email or social media.
Email: gina@ginaprosch.com
Follow This Days Joy: www.facebook.com/thisdaysjoy